Seven Promises
for Every Woman

From *Embraced by God*

Babbie Mason

Abingdon Press
Nashville

Seven Promises for Every Woman
From *Embraced By God*
Copyright © 2012 by Abingdon Press

This book is printed on acid-free paper.

ISBN 978-1-4267-5774-7

Scripture quotations marked ASV are from the American Standard Version of the Bible.

Scripture quotations marked CEB are from the Common English Bible. Copyright © 2011 by the Common English Bible. All rights reserved. Used by permission. www.CommonEnglishBible.

Scripture quotations marked KJV are from the authorized (King James) version. Rights in the Authorized Version in the United Kingdom are vested in the Crown. Reproduced by permission of the Crown's patentee, Cambridge University Press.

Scripture quotations from *THE MESSAGE*. Copyright © by Eugene H. Peterson 1993, 1994, 1995, 1996, 2000, 2001, 2002. Used by permission of NavPress Publishing Group.

Scripture quotations marked NIV are from the Holy Bible, New International Version®. Copyright © 1973, 1978, 1984, 2011 by Biblica, Inc.™ All rights reserved worldwide. www.zondervan.com. The "NIV" and "New International Version" are trademarks registered in the United States Patent and Trademark Office by Biblica, Inc. ™

Scripture quotations marked NKJV are taken from the New King James Version®. Copyright © 1982 by Thomas Nelson, Inc. Used by permission. All rights reserved.

Scripture quotations marked NLT are taken from the *Holy Bible*, New Living Translation, copyright © 1996, 2004, 2007. Used by permission of Tyndale House Publishers, Inc., Carol Stream, Illinois 60188. All rights reserved.

Scripture quotations marked NRSV are from the New Revised Standard Version of the Bible, copyright 1989, Division of Christian Education of the National Council of the Churches of Christ in the United States of America. Used by permission. All rights reserved.

Library of Congress Cataloging-in-Publication Data on file

12 13 14 15 16 17 18 19 20 21 — 10 9 8 7 6 5 4 3 2 1

MANUFACTURED IN THE UNITED STATES OF AMERICA

Contents

Introduction

Have you ever pondered, *Does God really love me? Does He accept me unconditionally? Is He concerned about my problems? Do I really matter to Him?*

If these thoughts have ever crossed your mind, take comfort; you are not alone. You join millions of people who, throughout the ages, have asked these same questions. I can admit that I have joined these ranks, and I've been a Christian most of my life. In fact, I was raised in church. I'm a preacher's daughter turned Christian singer, songwriter, and recording artist. Still, I have dealt with these very thoughts at different points during my life's journey . . . and I have learned, though at times my mind may wonder, God's love for me never changes.

If you sometimes question God's love for you, consider this: I believe God places these longings in us to create a hunger for Him. I believe we long to be with Him and desire to be loved completely by Him so that we will stay in His presence—where He desires for us to be.

I accepted Christ when I was eight years old, and in another year I will celebrate what I call my "Year of Jubilee," fifty years of knowing Christ as my Lord and Savior. Yet just a couple of years ago my eyes were opened to a new awareness of God's love when I heard my good friend Dr. Tony Ashmore, pastor of the Life Gate Church in Villa Rica, Georgia, preach a life-changing sermon. On that Sunday morning he instructed each person in the congregation to turn to one's neighbor and say, "I am God's favorite."

My friend's words troubled me at first. Initially I thought, *How could I be God's favorite? I have a past filled with mistakes. I have issues and challenges in my life. There are so many people who must stand ahead of me in line for that prize.*

Don't get me wrong. I have always known that God loves me, and honestly speaking, just knowing this was enough for me. I was satisfied with that. But to consider that I could *ever* be God's favorite? That seemed to be overstepping a boundary, even a bit presumptuous. I reasoned to myself that if God had favorites, then I certainly couldn't be one of them. This motivated me to seek God and the truth of His word. As I studied the Scriptures, two passages stood out to me. In John 17:22-23 (NLT), Jesus said,

> I have given them the glory you gave me, so they may be one as we are one. I am in them and you are in me. May they experience such perfect unity that the world will know that you sent me and that you love them as much as you love me.

Romans 8:17a adds, "Since we are his children, we are his heirs. In fact, together with Christ we are heirs of God's glory" (NLT).

Suddenly, God quickened my heart. I realized that God not only loves me but He loves me just as much as He loves His own Son, Jesus. I also became more deeply aware that everything God gave to Jesus, He has also given to me! These realizations have taken my love relationship with God to another level and made me more keenly aware of His loving presence and purpose in my life. I have concluded that if I, a Christian for nearly fifty years, could come to a profoundly new understanding of God's love, then maybe you could too. The promises in this little book are part of the fruit of that discovery.

As we prepare to encounter God's amazing love together, I want to serve as your trusted friend, encouraging you along the way, for I am someone whose life has been transformed by the power of God's amazing love. My prayer is that you, too, will be changed as you realize that God not only loves you, He loves you passionately and completely. He loves you without condition and without exception. He loves you as much as He loves Jesus. As a matter of fact—you are His favorite as well. You see, this is not a message of favoritism for a select few. This love is for all of God's children. As you draw near to Him, you will experience your own unique place in His favor and grace. Your heavenly Father desires to have a deep and intimate relationship with you through His Son, Jesus Christ, and He wants His love to impact every area of your life. No matter what you are facing at this moment, He wants to embrace you: in your challenges, victories, or defeats, and in your strengths, weaknesses, or fears.

The promises in this book have to do with this amazing, unconditional, passionate love of God. Here are the seven wonderful promises:

- You are loved unconditionally by God.
- You are beautiful to God.
- You are never alone.
- You have everything you need in God.
- You have a God-given purpose.
- You can accomplish great things in God's name.
- You are equipped with unique gifts and talents.

Before you begin reading about these promises, give God permission to transform your thinking and change any misconceptions you have about Him, or yourself. You will learn many new things about your loving heavenly Father, and you may even make some new discoveries about who you are. These seven promises will help you to understand with more clarity who you are in God and who He is in you.

Are you ready? Let's get started!

1

You Are Loved Unconditionally by God

God loves you and finds great pleasure and delight in you.

Imagine the most wonderful love relationship you could ever experience here on earth. Envision a love without limits or conditions. Consider a relationship that is completely satisfying in every way; *now* visualize the height of this relationship and multiply that as high as you can count. If you could count all the way to infinity and beyond, your answer would still be far too small compared to how much God really loves you. His love for you is passionate, unconditional and far, far, beyond any love you could ever experience with another human being.

Your heavenly Father wants you to see yourself as He sees you—loved beyond your capacity to imagine, saved from your sins, healed from all diseases, delivered from bondages, and free to live the life He has planned for you. As you take hold of this life-changing truth it will impact the way you think and ultimately the way you live. Not only does the God of the universe love you; He wants more than anything for you to love Him in return. And the more you reflect on God's amazing love, the more you will do just that.

As you think about God's unconditional love for you, consider three incredible truths.

You are God's favorite.

That's right: you are God's favorite—just like every other child of God. God sees each of His children and loves them completely and shows them His favor. We are God's favored ones—His "favor-ites." God quickened my heart and showed me that not only does He love me but He loves me just as much as He loves His own Son, Jesus.

It's hard to grasp how a holy, perfect, infinite God could ever love sinful, unholy, imperfect, and finite people, but He does. The Bible says that God even loved us first, before we knew anything about love or were capable of love—"This is love, not that we loved God, but that he loved us" (1 John 4:10a NIV).

Our understanding of love is so different than the way God loves us. You see human love is temperamental, temporary, and tentative. God's love, on the other hand, is constant, eternal, unabashed, and overflowing. While we know about love, we cannot know the fullness of love until we get to know the one who *is* Love Himself.

God's love is perfect and meets us where we are—the good and the bad, the strengths and the weaknesses—and He loves us just the same. His love is perfect and extraordinary in every way. *You* are God's favorite. Don't just hear this with your ears; embrace it with your heart.

You can start again.

It doesn't matter who you are or what your story may be. Jesus will forgive every mistake, and He can satisfy every longing you have, if you ask Him. Everybody can use a do-over every now and then: another opportunity to get things right with the Lord. Life in Christ is the only road to discovering what true life really is. Jesus promises the forgiveness you need, the peace you long for, the acceptance you crave, and the love you desperately hunger for.

God knows your story and chooses you anyway! God will help you and give you not only a second chance but a third or fourth, or as many as you need to get it right. Your brand-new start is just a prayer away.

Talk to God and ask the Lord to free you from any guilt you carry about a "past life." Invite the Lord to shine His purifying light into the secret places in your heart and overcome even the most hidden sins. Remember that "if any man be in Christ, he is a new creature: old things are passed away; behold, all things are become new" (2 Corinthians 5:17 KJV).

You matter to God.

You are of great significance to God. You are not an accident or an afterthought. You are not illegitimate, a mistake, a slipup, or an "oops." Everything that God made, He made for a reason *and* said it was "good." This includes you.

Long before you were a gleam in your father's eye you were fashioned in the heart of God. Jeremiah 1:5a says, "Before I formed you in the womb I knew you, before you were born I set you apart" (NIV).

Everything about you is important to God. He is interested in each intricate detail of your life. If something matters to you, then it matters to God. Your relationships, finances, and job situations are of utmost concern to Him. Your health problems, family concerns, and apprehensions for the future all matter to God. You may feel unimportant or even insignificant, but God says you have *always* been important and significant. Read the truth of God's word in Ephesians 1:4-5:

> Even before he made the world, God loved us and chose us in Christ to be holy and without fault in his eyes. God decided in advance to adopt us into his own family by bringing us to himself through Jesus Christ. This is what he wanted to do, and it gave him great pleasure. (NLT)

God sees you through His perfect eyes of love. Though at times He will correct you when and if you veer off track, He does so with loving restoration in mind. God sees you, my friend. He knows your name. And you matter to Him more than you know.

Dear heavenly Father,

Thank You for helping me understand more clearly just how much You love me and that Your love is greater than all my faults. Knowing that I am your favorite and that I matter to You brings me a great deal of comfort, joy, and security. I am so grateful that You are the God of second chances. This new day is a gift from You, and I thank You for another opportunity to walk in your love—another opportunity to please you with my life. Forgive me for trying to fix things on my own. I'm appealing to You, gracious Father. I desperately need You now. I always have needed You; I just didn't know how much until now. I don't want You to be an outsider or stranger in my life. Like the great hymn writer Frances Ridley Havergal said, "Take my life and let it be, consecrated, Lord, to Thee." I make You first priority in my life. Please take Your rightful place. Once again, Lord, thank You. In Jesus' name, Amen.

2

You Are Beautiful to God

*Everything God made is beautiful,
including you.*

When God created the heavens and the earth and everything they encompassed, He proclaimed it was all good—and this includes you. How so? Before you were conceived in your mother's womb, you were in the mind of God. To Him, you will always be beautiful. You are His masterpiece.

There is no television commercial, magazine ad, or human opinion that can change this fact. You don't need anyone's approval or validation. The only thing that matters is what God says about you. If God says you are beautiful, favored, chosen, blessed, and free, then it is so. Now, it's time for you to believe it *completely*. From the very beginning you have been a part of God's great big, beautiful love story.

As you think about God's view of you, know that you are validated, vindicated, and valued.

You are validated.

God has placed His stamp of approval on your life. Have you ever been told things like these:

- You'll never amount to anything.
- You're ugly.
- You're a failure.
- You're a constant disappointment.

These verbal assaults and a host of others cut deep, right to the soul. Maybe one or both of your parents verbally abused you. Perhaps someone you looked up to, someone you really trusted, wounded you with careless words. And if you were told any of these things as a child, no doubt you remember specific and countless times and places when those verbal bombs were hurled at you.

Let me ask you a question in review. Who is the originator of these verbal assaults and the relentless, repetitive attacks you might be hearing over and over in your mind? You might say:

- My dad
- My mom
- My grandparents
- My teacher
- A coach
- My husband
- The bully on the playground

No, my friend, these people may be most immediately responsible for insulting you, but they are not the author of these destructive words. The enemy is the author of every attack, whether it is against your body, your mind, or your spirit. Remember the enemy is your adversary. He will do all he can to keep you from becoming everything God has destined you to be.

I truly believe our world is suffering from a love deficiency. Like the old song says, "Everybody needs love." Each and every soul needs love. We crave it. So many people today sense a void in their hearts, an acute emptiness that can only be satisfied by love.

So, where can you find *real love?* Lean in and listen closely. Love is not a warm and fuzzy feeling. Love is not an emotional urge or even a deep desire. Love is not feeling good about yourself or someone else. Love is not a sexual drive. Always remember, dear friend, that love is a person. That person is Jesus.

Right now, stop and think about the truth—not your feelings or the opinion of someone else wrapped in flesh—but the unchanging, undeniable, absolute truth. *The love you crave and long for is embodied in one person, Jesus Christ.* He is the only one who is both qualified and able to bring real love, meaning, and purpose to your life.

You are vindicated.

God also vindicates you. He sets you free from your past—from all accusation, allegation, guilt, and blame. Jesus is a master at fixing ruined lives, repairing busted families, mending broken hearts, and shoring up dashed dreams. Like no one else can do, Jesus takes damaged goods and gives them a new lease on life.

When a crowd of accusers brought a woman caught in adultery before Jesus and pressed Him to grant the stoning the law prescribed, He said to them, "He that is without sin among you, let him first cast a stone at her" (John 8:7b ASV). One by one they went away, from the oldest to the youngest. When He saw no one but her, He said to her, "Woman where are those thine accusers? hath no man condemned thee?" She replied, "No man, Lord." Jesus answered, "Neither do I condemn thee: go, and sin no more" (vv. 10b-11 ASV).

Jesus was the only person who was qualified to throw stones that day, yet He refused to lift a condemning hand against her. He genuinely cared for her soul. I don't know about you, but to know that Jesus does not condemn me, even though I'm guilty, unlocks the door to freedom and throws away the key.

Jesus is your defender. He is ready, willing, and able to vindicate you of any guilt and accusation. Romans 8:1 is a promise you can stand on: "There is therefore now no condemnation for those who are in Christ Jesus" (NRSV).

You are valued.

Jesus is not only your defender; He is your comforter. You can "give all your worries and cares to God, for he cares about you" (1 Peter 5:7 NLT). You are greatly valued.

When my husband, Charles, suffered a stroke, he was admitted to the hospital and taken straight to the intensive care unit. I refused to leave his beside. Each night I slept in the chair beside his bed, where he lay connected to wires and IVs. It seems that every dire situation has the potential to be magnified at night. As I sat in his room, reality set in and things looked bleaker in the dark hours after midnight. But I can attest to the fact that during those hours I felt God's presence more than at any other time I can remember. During those moments, the long hours when I cried and prayed, I found the Lord's presence to be the sweetest of all.

More than likely, you have cried many tears during your own long, dark nights. Perhaps you wondered if anyone cared; you might have even pondered if life was worth living. Friends are such a blessing, but they can go with you only so far, especially during times of deep trouble and distress. But praise the Lord, we do not ever have to go the distance alone. "God is our refuge and strength, a very present help in trouble" (Psalm 46:1 ASV).

Jesus understands exactly how you feel. He knows what concerns you during the day and what keeps you up late at night. Take refuge in Him. Nothing will build you up like being in the presence of God. Even at times when you don't seem to feel His presence, it's all right. Don't be led by what you feel. Be led by what you know is true. You are deeply loved by Jesus. Your life is worth more to Him than silver or gold. No matter what circumstances life may bring, look to Jesus to complete you and reveal your true identity.

Dear sweet Father,

I am so grateful that you have placed your seal of approval on my life. Thank you for healing my brokenness and meeting all my needs. I am grateful that Jesus is an advocate who has never lost a case; I can roll my guilt, shame, doubt, and every other dead weight I carry over on Him, because He cares for me. When I can trust no one else, I can share my deepest secrets with Him, knowing I will not be condemned. I praise Your name, merciful Father, that I can receive your grace and forgiveness for my sins and move on with my life. Hallelujah! Amen.

3

You Are Never Alone

Because God loves you, He will never leave or
abandon you. He recognizes your voice,
ever ready to attend to your needs as
only He can do.

What do you do when facing a difficult situation? Do you share your concern with a family member? Do you talk to a friend or get information from the Internet? Though at times each of these "earthly" options can aid you in your time of need, the best place to find life's answers is from the pages of God's word. And the only place you can find real love, unexplainable peace, and complete deliverance is in the arms of our loving Lord, Jesus. My dear friend, *He is able*. Jesus is just as close to you as the mention of His name. Amid the deafening voices of today's culture, you can still hear the voice of God: either as a still, small voice or one that resounds as deeply and widely as the sea. God is calling to you in an unmistakable way—through both His word and your everyday experiences—*so slow down and listen closely*.

As you think about God's presence with you, be assured that God is near, God hears, and God cares.

God is near.

God created us to enjoy good relationships: first with Him and also with others. You and I were created and called to enjoy God—to know Him and to make Him known. The reason we exist is to bring attention to Him, pointing all people and nations His way. My sweet friend, you were born to fellowship with God, bring Him pleasure with your life, and put His love on display. You must do so to such an extent that others will desire His love. When people see you, they should think of God and be absolutely convinced they cannot live another moment without Him.

It pleases God to call us His own. He desires our intimate companionship and friendship. A lot of people think they are a burden to God. Too many think they bother Him. Some believe that God is easily irritated and short-tempered. On the contrary, the Bible says that God is patient and longsuffering toward those He loves: "The Lord is not slack concerning his promise, as some men count slackness; but is longsuffering toward us, not willing that any should perish, but that all should come to repentance" (2 Peter 3:9 KJV).

When Jesus was walking on the earth, He was confined to being in one place at a time. But now we have the Holy Spirit, our dear Comforter who is constantly with us. Now, our Lord is everywhere *all the time*. Most important, He lives inside me and you. Once you have trusted the Lord Jesus as your Savior, you never have to be lonely again. His loving presence began to dwell in you the moment you asked Him to come into your heart. Because God loves you, He wants you to return His embrace and accept this gift of friendship. He desires you to reciprocate by coming into intimate fellowship with Him.

Recognize God's presence today through the Holy Spirit. Think deeply about His love for you as you take time to look around and inside you. When you look in the mirror, reflect on how wonderful it is to belong to Him. Everywhere you go, and with every breath you take, He is there.

God hears.

God desires to have an ongoing, loving, and life-giving conversation with you. In Jeremiah 33:3 we read, "Call unto me, and I will answer thee, and shew thee great and mighty things, which thou knowest not" (KJV). When the Creator of the universe speaks to you through His word and says, "Call unto me," He's giving you an open invitation to call Him. Just think about it. You have a direct line to talk with the God of the ages! That's what prayer is—talking to God.

Through the miracle of prayer, you can communicate with God—the King and Master of the universe—who loves you deeply. He's never too busy. You don't need to make an appointment. You won't get a busy signal or get put on hold. He promises that when you call, He will answer.

More than anything, God wants to be with you and help you with all your decisions. So take Him up on His invitation to bring all your requests before Him. Tell God the deepest secrets of your heart, and even more than this, take time to listen to Him. You can learn to recognize God's voice by reading the Bible, looking to the life of Jesus, and paying attention to your own experiences. And always remember that when you can't see God's hand, you can trust His heart.

God cares.

God is near to you, and He hears you because He loves you deeply. God cares so much for you that He will provide a haven, a safe place, for you to rest when challenges are wearing you down. It may seem that everything around you is falling apart, but hold on. God cares, and He'll make a way where there seems to be no way.

My dear friend, God is not aloof or distant concerning you, but wherever you are, He is there. God is not building a case against you. He has not put up His hand against you. On the contrary, God cares about everything that concerns you. God has stretched forth His hand against your enemies for your sake! *He is for you.* And if God is for you, what force in the heavens, what adversary on earth, and what demon from the depths below could come against you and prevail?

Let God fill you with a song of hope today!

Dear Father,

Thank you for promising never ever to leave or forsake me. I praise you and acknowledge that whatever I encounter today, you are already there. I am amazed how You can be everywhere at once, hear the prayers of all Your children, and answer each of us according to our own individual needs. Lord, teach me to rest in the fact that when I call, You will answer—when You want, how You want, and any way You want. I'll be satisfied because I believe You know what's best for me. I submit all my cares and concerns into your hands, and I trust that over time, I will continually see your faithfulness. Help me always to remember that you are near, you hear, and you care for me. Amen.

4

You Have Everything
You Need in God

*Because God loves you, you have the assurance
that He will provide everything you need.*

One of the most reassuring promises God has
ever given is that He would provide for us because
He loves us. No one can provide for you like the
Lord. He knows exactly *what you need* before
you even know you need it. He knows exactly
how to provide for your need because He owns
all heavenly and earthly resources. And only the
Lord knows *when you need it most*. I have heard
the following saying ever since I was a child. The
words still ring true today. "He may not come
when you want Him, but He's always right on
time!" In His perfect knowledge, power, and love,
God is able to supply all your needs "according to
his riches in glory by Christ Jesus" (Philippians
4:19 NRSV).

You can trust in God.

The Lord Jesus is the *only* One who is truly worthy of complete trust. He is sure, reliable, proved, consistent, and dependable. God watches over us in a very personal way, reassuring us time and again that He is on our side.

Proverbs 3:5-6 is the Bible's most classic passage about unwavering trust in God: "Trust in the LORD with all thine heart; and lean not unto thine own understanding. In all thy ways acknowledge him, and he shall direct thy paths" (KJV). To trust Jesus in the way the Father desires, it is essential for you to maintain an intimate, ongoing relationship with Him. You must get to know Him through His word and by spending daily time in prayer. Then when challenges come, you will let go of every fear and concern and fall into His arms, because it is impossible to worry and trust God at the same time. As you experience God's unfailing presence in your life, you will find that to know Him is to love and trust Him more and more.

God knows everything about you, understands every detail about your strengths and weaknesses, and is intimately acquainted with your hopes, dreams, and weaknesses. After all, He created you and placed them inside you. You can rely on His perfect wisdom. And as His word promises, He will direct your path.

You can depend on God.

Over and over again, we're reminded that miracles can happen in our lives because God is with us. This is the secret to our success. You could have it all by the world's standards, but if the Lord isn't on your side, you are fighting a losing battle. However, when you are committed to the work of the Lord, your battles become His. He will fight for you. You don't have to worry about when the Lord will overcome the enemy. You don't need to concern yourself about how God goes about His battle plan. You just have to rest in the fact that He will. "The LORD is my light and my salvation; whom shall I fear? The LORD is the strength of my life; of whom shall I be afraid?" (Psalm 27:1 KJV).

As you obey God's marching commands, keep trusting in His great love for you. It takes tremendous courage to keep marching on when you're uncertain how your situation is going to turn out. It takes bold, audacious faith in God to keep moving forward on His instructions, even when you feel He is keeping you in the dark.

Can you submit to God's plan while staring into the face of impossibility? As your life intersects with God's love today, ponder the battles that God has already won in your life. Now, see yourself victorious as you obey God's new and unique battle plan.

God *is* working. God *is* moving. There are moments in our lives where we just have to give Him time. Behind the scenes, God is taking what looks like chaos at first glance and sounds like absolute mayhem and turning it around. He is creating a beautifully orchestrated symphony, aligning all things in perfect harmony to work *for your good* and *for His glory*.

No matter what you're facing, there is always hope in God. So, be courageous! Have confidence in Him. Stand firm in your faith, boldly committed to the Lord, just as the scripture instructs:

Have not I commanded thee? Be strong and of a good courage; be not afraid, neither be thou dismayed: for the L○RD thy God is with thee whithersoever thou goest.

Joshua 1:9 KJV

God will faithfully provide for all of your needs as you obediently trust Him in every situation.

You can rest in God.

Whatever you need, you can come and receive it from Jesus right now—just like the thirsty woman at the well did in the days of old. Come, get as much as you need from Jesus. Get filled up and be completely satisfied in His presence. He is your ultimate source of everything you need in this life.

Jesus calls to you, "Come unto me, all ye that labour and are heavy laden, and I will give you rest" (Matthew 11:28 KJV). The Lord Jesus, by the presence of the sweet Holy Spirit, who is with you and alive in you, is calling you to a new life . . . a lifestyle of complete rest and peace. Exchange any heavy burdens you might bear for the light and easy love of Jesus. *Slow down. Take your time. Rest in His presence.* He is your ever-faithful provider.

Almighty God,

Sometimes it seems that the odds are against me. Some days I feel as if I'm fighting a losing battle, taking three steps forward and two steps back. And when I look at things with my natural eyes, it seems that everything in my world is falling apart. Sometimes I feel the pressures of life on every side, and when I look out ahead of me, all I can see is a massive wall. My life is full of speed bumps, potholes, detours, and delays, Lord. Sometimes my bill box is nearly full and my gas tank is nearly empty. If I didn't know any better during these tests of my faith, I'd think the whole world was turning against me. But I praise You that I do know better! I know that if You are for me, You are much greater than whatever is coming against me. So today, sweet Father, I ask for courage to stand when my knees are weak. I ask for confidence to carry out Your instructions, even when my mind can't make sense of them. And, Lord, I ask for a heart that is singularly committed to Your cause. I realize this is a dangerous request because asking this of

You potentially invites more drama into my life. But I know that when I am weak, You are strong. And depending on Your strength is where I want to be. I know it's just a matter of time until I cross over into Your promised land of victory in my life. I love You, Lord. In the name of Your Son, Jesus, I pray. Amen.

5

You Have a God-given Purpose

*Because God loves you and has a
great plan for your life,
you are already a success.*

You have been given only one opportunity to glorify God with your life. What are you doing with it? Some people drift like a boat without a sail, heading out to sea in deep, uncharted waters. But you must seize every moment, desiring to live each day to the fullest. It is God's will for you to enjoy a purposeful, satisfying life.

God has a plan for you.

As believers, we want to know how to find God's plan for our lives. Maybe you have been wondering, *Who will I marry?* Or *Should I take the job?* Perhaps you're in a season where you are pondering, *Should I go away to college or attend the community college across town?*

Maybe you are at a place in your life where you are deciding whether to buy or rent a home. Oh, yes, there are many questions in life. The good news is God wants you to know His will and purpose for your life more than you do. He doesn't play hide-and-seek.

Knowing God has always had a plan for you should bring you a great sense of security. And what a big plan it is! Your heavenly Father wants to show you how to maximize every moment He has given you. He wants you to get all you can out of life, all the days of your life.

You (yes, *you!*) can worship God and enjoy a prosperous, successful, and fulfilling lifestyle. And if you are anything like me, you relish the opportunity to do so! I want to enjoy a life that allows me to maximize my relationships with people, my work, my times of recreation, and most of all my relationship with God. So, when challenges come, they don't intimidate me. I know that God loves me and that He causes even my challenges to work out for, not against, me. No challenge is going to take me under. I am an overcomer in Christ!

God's plan for you is always the best plan. Remember: *Father knows best*. When you want to know anything about your life, *just ask Him*. God knows everything there is to know about you. *The God who created you has written your life story. He has a predetermined plan for you.*

Take a closer look at God's plan for you. I trust you will discover that, indeed, God has a wonderful plan that has touched every age and stage of your life. Jesus takes great delight in blessing you according to His plan. God has a specific plan for you to accomplish. As you seek and worship Him, you will be able to see His plan unfold. And as a result, you'll maximize your efforts. You'll discover what living the abundant life truly is all about.

Here's the bottom line. The Bible may not tell you specifically whom to marry, what job to take, or whether to rent or buy your home. But the word of God will always tell you how to tune your heart and align your life, so you can recognize God's ultimate best when you see it.

I'd like you to think about what I call "The Four Ws of Walking in His Purpose." Try to keep them closely in mind, today and every day:

To know God's will, devote your time to reading His WORD.

God's will is found in His word. Just like a car's navigation system acclimates to true north, revealing turn-by-turn instructions that lead to your destination, reading the Bible is your spiritual compass. It is where you find God's instructions to live a life that is pleasing to Him (Romans 12:2).

To know God's will, develop an intimate WALK.

Knowing God's plan for your life means first getting to know Him: the Author of the plan. Putting first things first, you must know God personally through His Son, Jesus Christ, to begin walking in His plan. Look at it this way. *No God, no purpose. Know God, know purpose.*

To know God's will, delight in His WAYS.

If you want to know the ways of God, look at the life of Jesus. Do you want to please God? Live like Jesus. Do you want to develop lifelong relationships and influence people? Lead like Jesus. Do you want to be a blessing to people and serve well? Love like Jesus.

To know God's will, dedicate your life through Worship.

Honor God by living a life of obedience. God is concerned about one thing—your love for and obedience to Him. Your daily life can be a wonderful act of worship if you live it to the glory of God (Romans 12:1 NIV).

Knowing that God has a plan for me always leaves my heart at peace. Regardless of what happens during my day, I can rest assured that my life is securely in God's hands. Today, trust that God's plan is at work in your life.

God is with you.

God not only has a plan for your life but He wants you to be successful in every area of your life. Oftentimes we think of success as prosperity and notoriety. Our culture measures success by accomplishments, awards, and applause. But the Bible gives us a completely different definition of success. According to God's word, success isn't wrapped up in possessions, fame, or recognition. Success is not determined by who you are. Real success is determined by who you are with. You are a success for one reason only—because the Lord Jesus is with you!

When you allow God's great love to influence who you are, there are no limits to what you can accomplish. Knowing God changes your life and destiny. Don't think for one moment that God can't use you. When you're feeling overwhelmed or inadequate, say the following passage from the book of Philippians. I call it the ten finger prayer. Raise both hands and count off each word as you recite it: "I can do all things through Christ who strengthens me" (Philippians 4:13 NKJV).

Regardless of your faults and foibles, God can and will use you to accomplish His purposes.

God gives you hope.

No matter what your present situation may seem to be, God promises your future is filled with hope: hope that is as bright as His deep love for you. A great big God is on your side. He wants to "open you the windows of heaven, and pour you out a blessing, that there shall not be room enough to receive it" (Malachi 3:10 ASV) as you follow His plan. In God, your future is brimming over with promise and pregnant with possibilities.

I am sure there have been times when things around you have appeared to be anything but hopeful. During these times it can be difficult to say there is hope. Let me assure you, there is good news! Because Jesus finished His perfect work at the cross, no matter what things may look like, we have a great hope and a bright future.

You may have a long list of challenges, but God loves you. God has already made a way for you. And He wants you to be assured by faith that hope is not just around the corner. *Hope is available to you right now.*

In Christ, you don't have to give up or give in to life's challenges. You can get filled up with His presence and believe for a turn-around, try again, start over. . . . Whatever the situation requires, you can do above and beyond that. Hope always rises above it all because God's grace is sufficient for your every need. His "power" is perfected in your weakness (2 Corinthians 12:9 NIV).

Whatever you may be facing, look to God and remember His hope-filled promises!

Hope in the LORD!
Be strong! Let your heart take courage!
Hope in the LORD!

Psalm 27:14 CEB

Awesome God,

You are so amazing! You have a plan for my life and are concerned about every detail of my life. There have been times I didn't understand the ways You were at work in my life, but, Lord, I know Your ways are perfect. Help me to trust you in every way and depend on you fully. Jesus, I want to use all that I have and all that I am to promote the kingdom of God and make Your name famous in the earth. Help me to define success by Your standards from this day forward. I understand that real success is found in You and You alone. Enable me to release every care, every burden, every broken dream in exchange for Your promise of a bright future. Give me guidance for my plans, grace for my weaknesses, love for my lack of charity, forgiveness for my sins, and acceptance for every time I have been rejected. Fill my heart with hope and top it all off with a relentless joy that overflows into every area of my life. In Jesus' name, Amen.

6

You Can Accomplish Great Things in God's Name

Because God loves me, He has given me the ability to do big things—all for His glory.

If you were given the choice to have a real diamond or a fake one, which would you choose? I don't know about you, but I would say, "Give me the real thing!" There's a popular saying going around that tells you to "fake it 'til you make it." I say with Jesus on your side, you are more than a conqueror, and there's no need to put up a front. Why fake it, only appearing to possess victory in Jesus, when you can have the bona fide, real deal? Celebrate God's great power that is available to you. This power—that equips you to make a difference, to do the right thing, or even to do the impossible—is *in Christ*, and He is *in you*.

We need the bona fide power of God in the world today. Because only His anointing equips us to complete the task to which He has called us. And only His mighty power can break every yoke of bondage. Only His love melody can penetrate a world gone crazy and bring light and life to hurting, wounded, wayward souls. Every symphony has a crescendo, when the music intensifies to a dramatic peak. It is the same in God's symphony of love. He loved the world so intensely that it peaked and He gave His only begotten Son. Jesus came, continued flowing in love, and it peaked wherever He went. People who were blind could see, people who were deaf could hear, and people who could not speak could speak again. Broken lives and hearts were mended. Even the dead rose from the grave.

The Father wants His children to keep flowing in His power, sharing His love in this lost and dying world. Because of God's great power at work in you, you have the ability to step out, rise up, and make a big difference in the world.

Step out.

God wants you to put your faith into practice. The story of the disciples' faith adventure, which took place in a violent storm on the Sea of Galilee, is powerful. Jesus appeared to His followers, calmly walking on the high, menacing waves. Thinking they had seen a ghost, the disciples cried out in fear. Jesus spoke to them, telling them not to be afraid. Peter, always the audacious one, shouted out, "Lord, if it is you, command me to come to you on the water" (Matthew 14:28b NJV). Jesus invited him to come, and Peter immediately stepped out of the boat. Peter walked on the water, but when he saw the wind was boisterous, he was afraid and began to sink. He cried out for Jesus to save him, and Jesus reached out and caught him.

Peter is often looked down upon because of his fear. But in my opinion, he deserves a standing ovation. While the other disciples cowered in the boat, Peter was the only one who dared to step out in faith, and he actually walked on water!

Peter is a shining example for us all. If you are going to follow Jesus, at some point you will have to leave familiar surroundings and the comfort of the crowd. Many times it is neither popular nor easy to step out in faith, and you must pray for the vision, wisdom, strength, and obedience to embrace your God-given assignment. When you step out in faith, some people will try to talk you out of obeying God. But listen to the One who calls your name above the noise of the crowd. And if you fail along the way, remember that Jesus has your back; with His help, you will be able to rise up just like Peter.

Rise up.

God's mighty power equips you to get back up as often as life's challenges knock you down.

God loves us so much that He always causes our challenges to work for us, not against us. In Christ, what may appear to be a setback is not a setback at all. *It is a setup for a comeback!* Every challenge is a launching pad for success. It's another opportunity to experience God's power in your life!

So, what's the process? How do we come back strong after a setback? *The first and most important step in the process, after being knocked down, is simply to get up.* Don't wallow in the mire and throw a pity party. No one will come to join you anyway. People just don't want to come to pity parties. Don't put on the cloak of guilt. That's one little black dress you don't even need to try on. Don't become paralyzed by fear. Realize what's happening, and look it square in the face. Self-pity, guilt, and fear are arrows that the enemy uses to wound your spirit and render you ineffective. Self-pity, guilt, and fear can disable you. Remember that satan is the great accuser. But Jesus offers loving forgiveness. When the Pharisees brought the woman caught in the act of adultery to Christ, He dismissed her accusers with a challenge for the one who was without sin to "first cast a stone at her" (John 8:7b KJV). Then He turned to the woman and reaffirmed her. Jesus did not condemn this woman, pronouncing her guilty or inflicting severe punishment on her. He simply said, "Neither do I condemn thee: go, and sin no more" (v. 11). Jesus exhorted her to get on with her life and stop the destructive behavior.

No self-pity. No guilt. No fear.

Today is a great day to stage a comeback, don't you agree? If life has dealt you a low blow, bringing you down to your knees, always remember—you don't have to stay down. With the help of God, you can rise up, brush yourself off, and press on.

Make a big difference.

By His great power, God has divinely shaped you to make an amazing difference in this world for His glory. In a world filled with violence, hatred, selfishness, pride, deception, and greed, as blood-bought believers in Jesus Christ, we are called upon to be salt and "season" this unsavory mix. He has given us the mission of making the world a little bit more like heaven on earth by sharing His love.

Jesus said, "Love your neighbor as yourself" (Luke 10:27 NIV), and then he told the parable of the good Samaritan, in which he not only *defined* neighbor but also painted a picture of love that transcends religious, ethnic, social, and racial divides, as well as educational and economic differences (Luke 10:30-37). In this story, Christ is telling us that, like the good Samaritan, as we journey through this life in our day-to-day experiences, we can take time from our busy schedules to become actively involved in the welfare of our neighbor. We can show concern. We can speak kind words. We can commit our resources. We can express *agape* love—selfless, unconditional love—to another person who, like us, has been created in the image of God.

Showing love is not complicated. Even small efforts can make a big difference with God in the equation. Opportunities are all around you, my friend. Turn to others and share the love of Christ.

Dear faithful Father,

I am so grateful that Your love for me is bigger than the challenges I face. I confess that sometimes I am overwhelmed by my circumstances. Forgive me for not trusting You. Thank you that I can exchange my doubts for faith and replace my fears with courage. Thank You for setting me free from self-pity, guilt, and fear. Without a doubt, I am loved, forgiven, fearless, and free. Help me to make a difference in this world by demonstrating the agape love of Christ to everyone I encounter. Amen.

7

You Are Equipped With Unique Gifts and Talents

Because God loves you, He has bestowed upon you gifts and talents to use for His glory. Make yourself available to Him.

God has equipped each of us with gifts and talents to accomplish His specific will and purpose for our lives with ease. There's nothing more fulfilling than traveling in the lane where you know you are assigned. When you are confident of God's call on your life, you will not be concerned about the gifts and talents of others. You will not be jealous or envious of their success, comparing yourself to them. Rather, you will find that you can celebrate them, instead.

God's promise within you is limitless, boundless, and inexhaustible. It's running over with power according to Ephesians 3:20. My friend, God will do "exceeding abundantly above" your greatest dreams, according to His mighty power that is at work within you. Just as a cook stirs a wonderful pot of flavorful homemade soup that's been simmering on low heat atop the back burner of the stove, the Lord desires to reach down to the bottom of your heart and stir your gifts from the bottom up, releasing all of your Godlike potential.

To participate in this amazing process, you must encourage your heart, equip your hands, and envision your future.

Encourage your heart.

Do you have deep disappointments that weigh heavily in your heart? Are you feeling the deep pain and sting of suffering a great loss? Take comfort, my friend. You don't have to wait for others to speak the encouraging words you long to hear. You can speak over yourself like David did in the Old Testament.

First Samuel 30:1-6 tells us that David and his troops returned home to Ziklag only to find everything they held dear completely wiped out by the Amalekites. When they found their homes smoldering in ruins and their loved ones gone, the Bible says these mighty men wept until they had no more power to weep. David had to endure the threat of his own troops turning against him in the wake of their grief. In spite of it all, the Bible tells us that "David encouraged himself in the LORD his God" (1 Samuel 30:6 KJV).

Though the enemy may attack us by stealth, doing his best to hit us hard and unexpectedly, hoping his wicked scheme of discouragement and depression will pull us under, *we only need to stand in faith and remember*—God has already gone before us and paved the way to victory. God is working all things together for our good—because we love Him and are "called according to his purpose" (Romans 8:28b NIV). Encourage yourself by looking back and reviewing your history with God. Reflect on the storms God has brought you through, recalling His faithfulness. Then remember and meditate on the promises of God. A great way to meditate on God's word is through self-talk, which is talking to yourself concerning your situation—rehearsing God's promises, not your problems. Keeping your mind on the Lord will cause you to be encouraged, productive, and fruitful.

Equip your hands.

Because God loves you, He has given you unique gifts and talents to do great things in His name. You are His masterpiece, pregnant with incredible promise to effect change in the world around you. God has placed you on the earth at just the precise time you are needed. God wants to use you! God loves you with a deep, abiding love. He has great plans for you. His plan is to prosper you, not to do you harm. He wants to fill your days with enduring hope. Anticpate the many ways He will use you in the days to come.

What has God uniquely equipped you to do? As we have discussed, God has a unique assignment for you. If you know what that assignment is, don't let fear, pride, pretense, or a need for approval get in your way. Rather, remember the Apostle Paul's encouraging words:

Whatever you do, work at it with all your heart, as working for the Lord, not for men, since you know that you will receive an inheritance from the Lord as a reward. It is the Lord Christ you are serving.

Colossians 3:23-24 NIV

You can accomplish great things for Christ because He has empowered you to do what He's called you to do. Your attitude as His child and willing servant should be one not of pressure or obligation, but of privilege. True servants don't say with dread, "Ugh! I have to do this." Instead, they say with joy, "Oh! I get to do this!" If you are still seeking God for your assignment, begin asking Him right now to give you opportunities and occasions to serve Him. John Wesley, a great preacher and a humble servant, lived by an incredible motto. Let his words motivate you to find God's assignment for your life and get to it. This is what he said:

> Do all the good you can,
> By all the means you can,
> In all the ways you can,
> In all the places you can,
> At all the times you can,
> To all the people you can,
> As long as ever you can.*

*George Eayrs, ed., *Letters of John Wesley: A Selection of Important & New Letters* (London: Hodder & Stoughton, 1915), p. 423.

Envision your future.

Your life is a reflection of who Christ is in you. The apostle Paul wrote, "I do not count myself to have apprehended; but one thing I do, forgetting those things that are behind and reaching forward to those things which are ahead, I press toward the goal for the prize of the upward call of God in Christ Jesus (Philippians 3:13-14 NKJV). He admitted that he was a work in progress—that we all are for that matter—and he admonished us to keep our eyes on the prize. On an ongoing basis, review your calling and constantly let God nudge you into the place you were meant to fit best. Make your Father's name famous in the earth. Without Christ you are nothing, but with Him you can do great things in His name.

This very moment could be a defining one if you allow it to be. You could close this book and say, "That was nice." Or, you could say, "That was then and this is now . . . and starting now, with the help of God, I will live like I know I'm God's favorite." From this moment forward you can know, beyond the shadow of any doubt:

- You are deeply loved by God, without condition.
- You are complete in Him, lacking nothing.
- You are never alone; God is with you.
- Your needs are all met because God has supplied them.
- You have a specific assignment to complete.
- You are equipped with power to carry out that assignment in God's name.
- Your God is faithful to complete the unique work He started in you.

Dear heavenly Father,

I thank You that even in my lowest moments, I need not look to anyone but You to supply my deepest need for encouragement. Help me to meditate on Your word instead of my circumstances. Remind me daily that I am uniquely equipped and filled with promise to shed Your love abroad in simple ways. Help me to overcome any fear or apprehension that could keep me from joyfully carrying out Your work and accomplishing great things in Your name. Amen.

Epilogue:

You Can Live *Loved*

Today is full of hope, promise, and new beginnings as a result of the life-changing truths you've encountered in these seven wonderful promises. The days to come will present you with many opportunities to act on these promises and start living *loved*. That simply means to be consciously aware of God's loving presence in your life—to live and love on purpose.

Remember that your love relationship with God is alive and active. It must be cultivated on a daily basis. You'll have to keep sowing the seeds of this love—and the more you sow, the more you'll grow.

As long as there are life and breath in your body, you have the call from Christ to keep growing—to grow deeper, richer, and fuller in God's love. Your growth will come from staying connected to God and His word. Before you can ever be effective in serving God publicly, you must practice His presence by serving Him privately. This is the mark of true maturity.

Keep walking in the love that God has for you. Some days you'll be tired. Other days you'll be disappointed or discouraged. On days like these, you'll just need to keep putting one foot in front of the other. See yourself as God sees you:

- loved beyond your capacity to imagine;
- saved from your sins;
- healed from all diseases;
- delivered from the bondages of sin;
- free to live the life God has planned for you.

Keep reminding yourself over and over again of who and whose you are. This exercise will impact the way you think and ultimately the way you live.

No matter what tomorrow may bring, remember that God loves you and there is no need to fear the future because God is already there. He will give you just what you need, exactly the way you need it, at the precise moment you need it. God loves you as if you were the only one to love. You are His favorite. May this truth forever rock your world. And as you live loved day by day, returning the loving embrace of the Father, may you never, ever be the same!

Embrace this God-life. Really embrace it, and nothing will be too much for you. This mountain, for instance, just say, "Go jump in the lake"—no shuffling or shilly-shallying—and it's good as done. That's why I urge you to pray for absolutely everything, ranging from small to large. Include everything as you embrace this God-life, and you'll get God's everything.

Mark 11:22-24 *THE MESSAGE*

If you liked this book, you'll love the women's study.

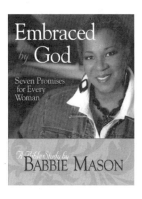

Experience Embraced by God: Seven Promises for Every Woman in a community of women as you study, share, and worship together. This eight-week program includes a book for every member, a leader guide, and a DVD featuring Babbie teaching and performing original music in her home.

Abingdon Press / August 2012

For more information about the study and Embraced by God Program Kit (UPC: 843504033927), visit **AbingdonPress.com** or your favorite Christian retailer.

Combining Christian Fiction and Bible Study

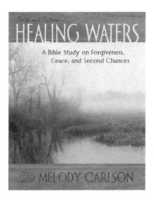

Popular Christian fiction author Melody Carlson draws upon her novels in the Inn at Shining Waters Series to invite women on an exciting journey toward healing. Using the stories, themes, and characters of the novels as a backdrop, this eight-week study explores the need for forgiveness and mercy in our lives and the role that second chances and new beginnings play in healing our spirits and relationships.

Abingdon Press / August 2012

For more information
visit **AbingdonPress.com**
or your favorite Christian retailer.